GREAT EXPEDITIONS

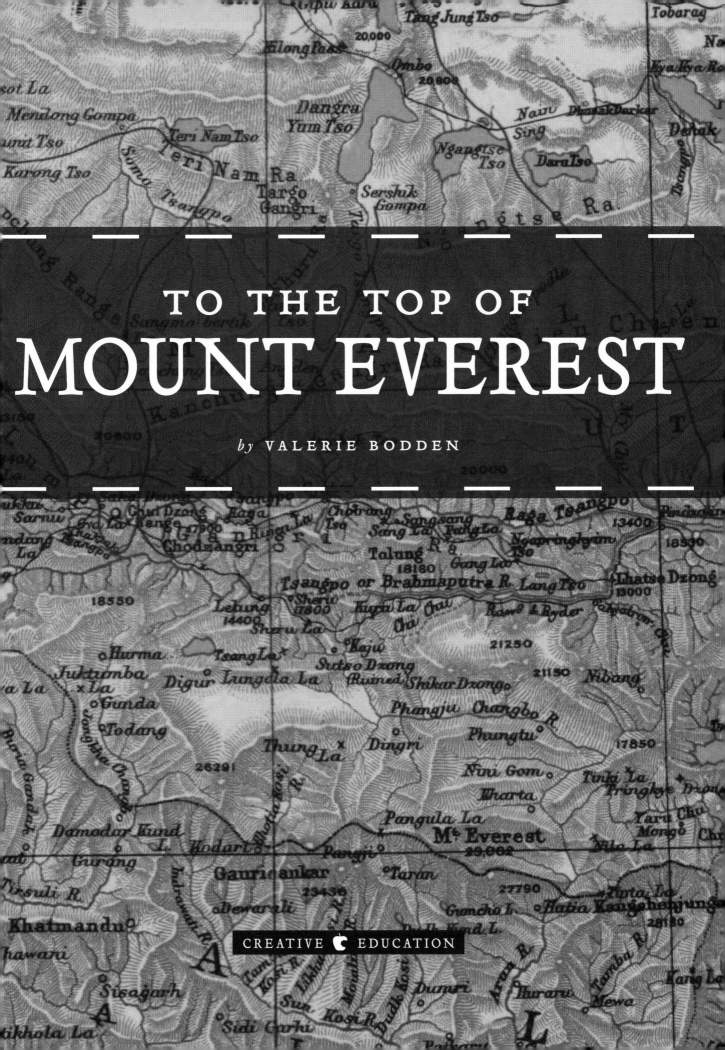

TO THE TOP OF
MOUNT EVEREST

by VALERIE BODDEN

CREATIVE EDUCATION

PUBLISHED BY Creative Education
P.O. Box 227, Mankato, Minnesota 56002
Creative Education is an imprint of The Creative Company
www.thecreativecompany.us

DESIGN AND PRODUCTION BY Ellen Huber
ART DIRECTION BY Rita Marshall
PRINTED BY Corporate Graphics
in the United States of America

PHOTOGRAPHS BY
Alamy (Royal Geographical Society), Corbis (Association Chantal Mauduit Namaste,
Hulton Deutsch Collection, Galen Rowell, STR/Keystone),
Getty Images (AFP, Express Newspapers, Keystone, Roger Mear, Matt Olson,
Popperfoto, Fred Ramage/Keystone, Three Lions),
The Granger Collection, NYC (Ullstein Bild), iStockphoto (Mike Bentley, Brandon
Laufenberg), Library of Congress, Royal Geographical Society

LIBRARY OF CONGRESS CATALOGING-IN-PUBLICATION DATA
Bodden, Valerie.
To the top of Mount Everest / by Valerie Bodden.
p. cm. — (Great expeditions)
Includes bibliographical references and index.
Summary: A history of Edmund Hillary and Tenzing Norgay's 1953 summit of
Mt. Everest, detailing the challenges encountered, the individuals involved, the discoveries made,
and how the expedition left its mark upon the world.

ISBN 978-1-60818-070-7
1. Hillary, Edmund, 1919–2008—Juvenile literature. 2. Tenzing Norkey,
1914–1986—Juvenile literature. 3. Mountaineers—Everest, Mount
(China and Nepal)—Biography—Juvenile literature.
4. Mountaineering—Everest, Mount (China and Nepal)—History. I. Title.

GV199.92.H54B63 2011
796.5220922—dc22 2010033553
CPSIA: 110310 PO1383

First Edition
2 4 6 8 9 7 5 3 1

TABLE of CONTENTS

Chapters
Chomolungma *7*
To Base Camp *17*
Up the Mountain *27*
On Top of the World *35*

1953 Everest Expedition Profiles
Edmund Hillary *13*
Tenzing Norgay *23*
John Hunt *33*
Tom Bourdillon *41*

Expedition Journal Entries
"An Admirable Companion" *9*
"No Longer Just a Dream" *19*
"Nothing Would Stop Us" *29*
"Our Band of Thirteen" *37*

Timeline *44*
Endnotes *45*
Selected Bibliography *46*
For Further Reading *47*
Index *48*

CHOMOLUNGMA

OR HUNDREDS OF YEARS, PEOPLE HAVE CLIMBED MOUNTAINS OUT OF NECESSITY, TO GET FROM ONE PLACE TO ANOTHER. BUT DURING THE 18TH CENTURY, ADVENTURERS IN EUROPE BEGAN TO SCALE MOUNTAINS FOR SPORT, AND SOON PEAKS AROUND THE WORLD WERE BEING SUMMITED. IT WAS NOT UNTIL THE 1920S, HOWEVER, THAT MOUNTAINEERS BEGAN TO

set their sights on the highest mountain in the world: Mount Everest. Located on the border of Nepal and Tibet, this 5.5-mile-high (8.9 km) peak had defeated climbers for more than 30 years before New Zealander Edmund Hillary and Nepalese Sherpa Tenzing Norgay stood on its summit in 1953. The "roof of the world" had finally been reached.

For more than four centuries before Hillary and Tenzing successfully summited Everest, Tenzing's people, the Sherpas, had lived in its foothills. The Sherpas, whose name means "eastern people," had migrated from Tibet to a region of northeastern Nepal known as Solu-Khumbu in the 15th century. Here, at the foot of Everest, a

Trekking through the Himalayas was a common, everyday occurrence for the Nepalese people before the advent of professional climbing.

mountain they called Chomolungma (meaning "mother goddess of the world" or "goddess of the valley" in Tibetan), Sherpas grew potatoes and barley and raised yaks for the animals' milk and hides. Although their crops were planted at altitudes of up to 14,000 feet (4,267 m), and they took their yaks as high as 17,000 feet (5,182 m) to graze, Sherpas did not climb the great peaks of the Himalayas before Europeans arrived. Informed by the most ancient traditions of Tibetan BUDDHISM, they believed that the mountains were the homes of gods and goddesses. Chomolungma itself was known as the home of the goddess Miyolangsangma, whom the Sherpas believed offered good fortune and wealth.

The 1921 British expedition to Everest was famous climber George Mallory's first attempt at finding a route to the mountain's summit.

The lamas (Buddhist monks, or spiritual leaders) of Solu-Khumbu warned that climbing the mountains would bring bad luck from the gods.

The first people to consider scaling Mount Everest were the British, who SURVEYED India and the Himalayas during the mid-19th century and discovered that, at 29,002 feet (8,840 m), Everest was the highest mountain in the world. (Subsequent measurements have shown that the mountain is even higher—29,035 feet, or 8,850 m.) In 1921, the British mounted their first expedition to Everest, although they could not approach the mountain from Solu-Khumbu, since Nepal was closed to foreigners at the time. Instead, they attempted to find a route up the mountain from Tibet, to the north, which had granted

EXPEDITION JOURNAL

Edmund Hillary
April 26, 1953

After a couple of hours Tenzing and I departed [Camp

IV] for Base Camp. We reached Camp III in one hour....

We descended to Camp II in 33 minutes on a perfect track.

We met George Lowe with a team of porters at II and

had a pleasant yarn.... Tenzing and I left Camp II with

a great rush which was suddenly checked when under the

weight of a hearty jump from me a large ice block sheared

off and descended with me down a crevasse. Only lively

work with my flailing CRAMPONS and a fortunately quick

rope from Tenzing stopped an unfortunate experience.

We continued to Base in 55 minutes. Tenzing is an admirable

companion—fit, energetic, capable and with excellent

rope technique.

them permission to climb. As they worked on scaling the north side, the climbers came to a high pass from which they were able to look down on the southern, or Nepalese, side of the mountain. What they saw—towering blocks of ice, yawning abysses, and steep slopes—led them to declare that Everest was impassable from that direction.

The 1921 British expedition marked the first time that Sherpas climbed Mount Everest for pay. Since the early 1900s, Sherpas had been working as porters, carrying loads in and out of the mountains for British expeditions in the region, and many had moved to Darjeeling, India, the departure point for Himalayan expeditions. This expedition to Everest—like all those to come—required porters to carry supplies and equipment to the remote mountain. Having lived in the Himalayas all their lives, Sherpas were well-adapted to carry out such demanding work.

The yak is a large, wild ox native to high-altitude Tibet that is often used for transporting heavy items up and down the mountainsides.

The goal of the 1921 British expedition was not to summit Everest but to explore potential routes to the peak. The next year, another British expedition set out for the mountain, this time with the goal of reaching the top. Although it did not succeed, two members of the party made it to 27,300 feet (8,321 m), higher than anyone had ever ascended on any mountain on Earth. The 1922 expedition also saw the first deaths on Everest, as seven Sherpas were killed in an avalanche. Tragedy marked the next British expedition, in 1924, as well, when climbers George Mallory and Andrew Irvine disappeared near the summit. (Mallory's body would not be found until 1999.) Before their disappearance, fellow climber Edward Norton had reached a record altitude of 28,100 feet (8,565 m), less than 1,000 feet (305 m) from the summit. During the 1930s, four more British groups made attempts on Everest, but none of them managed to surpass Norton's record.

With the onset of World War II in 1939, attempts to summit Everest were put on hold, and there were no expeditions for the next 10 years. By the time mountaineers were ready to return to Everest, Tibet had been taken over by China and its borders closed to WESTERNERS. At the same time, a revolution in Nepal had opened that country to foreigners again. As a result, anyone wanting to scale Everest now had to do so from the south. In 1950, a small party of British and American climbers traveled to Nepal to evaluate the possibility of finding a southern route up the mountainside. What they saw led them to agree

Mountaineers who attempted Everest in the early 1900s were often familiar with other tall peaks, such as France's Aiguille Verte.

1953 EVEREST EXPEDITION PROFILE: EDMUND HILLARY

Edmund Hillary was born in Auckland, New Zealand, on July 20, 1919, and grew up in the small town of Tuakau. He got his first taste of the mountains at age 16 during a trip to New Zealand's Mount Ruapehu. After two years studying math and science at the University of Auckland, Hillary dropped out to join his father's beekeeping business. In 1950, he traveled to the European Alps, and in 1951, he made his first trip to the Himalayas. After summiting Mount Everest, Hillary made expeditions to other Himalayan mountains, as well as to Antarctica and the North Pole. In 1960, he founded the Himalayan Trust to help improve the lives of Sherpas in Nepal, and he continued to work with the trust until his death in January 2008.

with the findings of the 1921 expedition: it was likely impossible to ascend this side of Everest.

Undeterred, the British sent a RECONNAISSANCE mission to Everest in 1951. This time, an energetic New Zealander named Edmund Hillary joined the expedition. Peering at Everest from the slopes of a nearby mountain, Hillary and expedition leader Eric Shipton were able to pick out a potential route to the top. The expedition eventually managed to scale Everest's first obstacle, a region of precariously balanced ice blocks and deep chasms known as the Khumbu Icefall. The team was confident that the next year it would reach the summit.

Eric Shipton, a veteran of the 1930s Everest expeditions (pictured opposite), was chosen to lead the 1951 trek but was passed over in 1953.

The expedition was not to have a chance, however. Although only the British had been granted access to Everest up to that point, in 1952, Nepal gave Switzerland permission to mount the only two expeditions of the year. Tenzing Norgay (who had been a porter for three of the British attempts during the 1930s) accompanied both Swiss expeditions. On the first, he and Swiss climber Raymond Lambert reached about 28,000 feet (8,534 m) before turning back. On the second expedition, faced with fierce winds and deadly cold, they didn't make it even that far. That meant there was still a chance for the British to be the first to summit the mountain. As a new team headed to Everest in the spring of 1953, their odds looked better than ever, as joining the expedition were two Everest veterans—Hillary and Tenzing.

To Base Camp

Like all previous British expeditions to Everest, the 1953 expedition was sponsored by the Himalayan Committee (formerly known as the Everest Committee), a joint venture of Great Britain's Royal Geographical Society and Alpine Club. In September 1952, the committee invited 42-year-old John Hunt, a colonel in the

British army, to lead the expedition. Although Hunt had never been on Everest, he had taken part in previous expeditions in other parts of the Himalayas. He accepted the invitation and quickly set about selecting expedition members. He wanted men between the ages of 25 and 40 who were strong and had experience climbing snow and ice.

Edmund Hillary, then 33 years old, fit the requirements exactly, as he was known to be a strong climber with a wealth of experience on the snow- and ice-covered mountains of New Zealand. He had also scaled a number of Himalayan peaks, in addition to taking part in the 1951 reconnaissance mission to Everest. Fellow

Cameraman Tom Stobart's inclusion in the 1953 expedition proved to be invaluable, as he was able to capture much of the action on film.

New Zealander George Lowe was also invited to join the expedition. Other team members included British climbers Charles Evans, Tom Bourdillon, Alfred Gregory, Michael Ward, Charles Wylie, George Band, Michael Westmacott, and Wilfrid Noyce, along with cameraman Tom Stobart, physiologist Griffith Pugh, and reporter James Morris.

Joining the group as sirdar, or leader of the Sherpa porters, would be Tenzing, on his seventh expedition to the mountain. (In addition to joining the British and Swiss expeditions, he had also led an illegal attempt by Canadian-born Earl Denman in 1947.) Unlike most Sherpas, Tenzing climbed not only for money

Michael Westmacott (left) first experimented with the use of oxygen systems while climbing in Great Britain and the Alps.

but also for the joy of climbing, and he was determined to finally get to the top of Everest. As sirdar, Tenzing hired hundreds of porters to carry supplies to the lower slopes, along with 20 climbing Sherpas to help transport equipment to camps higher up the mountain.

With the team selected, each member's thoughts turned to how he would survive in Everest's extreme conditions. Because the mountain is the highest in the world, one of the biggest factors affecting the expedition's performance would be the altitude. Differences in AIR PRESSURE make the air "thinner," or less dense, at high altitudes than it is at sea level. Although all air on Earth is made up of 21 percent oxygen, in thinner air, the oxygen MOLECULES are more spread out, so a person breathes in less oxygen with each breath. This creates a condition in the body known as hypoxia, or oxygen deprivation. If climbers increase their altitude slowly, their bodies can usually adjust, or acclimatize, to the altitude, but insufficient acclimatization can lead to headaches, nausea, fatigue, shortness of breath, or life-threatening CEREBRAL EDEMA. Even with a proper acclimatization period, the body never fully adjusts to altitudes above about 21,000 feet (6,400 m)—still a mile and a half (2.4 km) below Everest's summit—making even the act of putting one foot in front of the other a strenuous task. The thin air also affects the brain's ability to think clearly.

EXPEDITION JOURNAL

Tenzing Norgay
May 29, 1953 (from his 1955 autobiography Tiger of the Snows*)*

Many times I think of that morning at Camp Nine. We have spent the night there, Hillary and I, in our little tent at almost 28,000 feet, which is the highest that men have ever slept. It has been a cold night. Hillary's boots are frozen, and we are almost frozen too. But now in the gray light, when we creep from the tent, there is almost no wind. The sky is clear and still. And that is good. We look up. For weeks, for months, that is all we have done. Look up. And there it is—the top of Everest. Only it is different now: so near, so close, only a little more than a thousand feet above us. It is no longer just a dream, a high dream in the sky, but a real and solid thing, a thing of rock and snow, that men can climb. We make ready. We will climb it.

In order to help them deal with the extremely high altitudes they would be facing on Everest, the members of the expedition would use supplementary oxygen—carried in tanks on their backs—when scaling the highest mountain slopes. Although the oxygen wouldn't completely eliminate the effects of altitude, it would allow the climbers to work more efficiently, think more clearly, and even stay warmer. For the 1953 expedition, three types of oxygen systems were ordered: open-circuit (in which oxygen is blown across the face to supplement the surrounding air), closed-circuit (in which pure oxygen is breathed through a mask), and sleeping sets (worn at night to help climbers get more rest).

Expedition members had to wear many articles of protective clothing, in addition to regular climbing gear and oxygen support.

Along with a lack of oxygen, the expedition would face frigid weather conditions on Everest's high slopes, where temperatures regularly plunge well below 0 °F (-17.8 °C), and winds often blow at more than 100 miles (161 km) per hour year round. Clothing for such conditions included wool underclothing, shirts, and sweaters; down pants and jackets; and an outer, windproof covering, along with three pairs of gloves and lightweight, well-insulated boots. The expedition members' tents were made of wind-resistant material, and their double-layer sleeping bags were filled with down.

Climbing gear such as crampons, ropes, and ice hammers and axes would help the climbers get up the mountainside, and radios would allow them to monitor weather reports. Food for the expedition included biscuits, jam, cheese, soup, cocoa, and lemonade powder, as well as a few "luxury" items, such as tinned fruit and meat. Portable stoves were taken to heat the food and to melt snow for water.

By March 1953, the expedition's 18 tons (16.3 t) of gear and food had been sent to Kathmandu, Nepal's capital city, where the climbers gathered to begin their journey. After sorting through the equipment and piling it onto the backs of the 350 porters, the expedition set out on March 10 for the base of Mount Everest, nearly 200 miles (322 km) away. For 17 days, they traveled through the high ridges and deep valleys of northern Nepal, following rocky paths over mountain passes, crossing raging rivers on rickety hanging bridges, and trekking through forests of tall trees, fragrant flowers, and colorful birds.

On March 25, the expedition arrived in Namche Bazar, the largest Sherpa village, and then proceeded on to Tengboche Monastery. Located at an elevation of 12,700 feet (3,871 m), Tengboche offered an amazing view of Everest. Although the mountain's lower slopes were hidden by the neighboring peaks of Nuptse and Lhotse, its summit towered above all the other mountains. A plume of windblown snow could be seen unfurling from its highest reaches.

The expedition set up a temporary base at Tengboche, and the party spent the next three weeks climbing to around 20,000 feet (6,096 m) on several of the region's lower peaks in order to practice with the equipment and acclimatize before going higher. In early April, Hunt asked Hillary, Lowe, Band, and Westmacott to forge ahead and establish Camp I, or Base Camp, on the Khumbu GLACIER at the bottom of Everest. The group ascended to 17,900 feet (5,456 m) and set up camp on a relatively flat area of rock and ice. Then they prepared for the real work ahead.

1953 EVEREST EXPEDITION PROFILE: TENZING NORGAY

Born in May 1914, Tenzing Norgay was the 11th of 13 children.

He grew up in the Sherpa village of Thami in the Khumbu

region of Nepal. There was no school in Khumbu, so Tenzing

spent his time helping his father tend their yaks. In 1932, at

the age of 18, he moved to Darjeeling, India, where he became

a porter for Himalayan expeditions. He took part in his first

Everest expedition in 1935 and embarked on five more trips

up the mountain before successfully reaching the summit in

1953. In 1954, Tenzing joined the newly established Himalayan

Mountaineering Institute, where he worked as director of field

training until 1976. Afterward, he became a guide for trekking

expeditions in Nepal and nearby countries. Tenzing died in 1986.

To the east of
Mount Everest
is the fifth-highest
peak in the world
(at 27,766 feet,
or 8,463 m),
Mount Makalu,
which was first
ascended in 1955.

Up the Mountain

Because a mountain as large as Everest couldn't be climbed in a single day, the plan for reaching the summit was to set up a series of eight camps at progressively higher altitudes, with a final, ninth camp close enough to the summit that the remaining distance could be covered in a day. Hunt arranged the schedule so that the expedition members would take turns with the hardest work, such as establishing new routes. That way, while some worked on the mountain and slept at the higher camps, the others could carry supplies between camps and spend at least some evenings at the lower camps to keep their bodies in better shape.

It fell to Hillary, along with Westmacott, Band, and Sherpa Ang Namgyal, to forge a route up the Khumbu Icefall. Though Hillary had previously scaled the icefall in 1951, he found it much changed. Huge ice towers had tumbled and shifted, and new crevasses, or cracks, had opened in the ice. Although Hillary thought the icefall looked almost impassable, he

The success of the expedition can be credited in large part to the Sherpas who worked tirelessly to transport all the necessary supplies.

and his team managed to establish a route through it in five days, cutting steps into the ice and fastening ropes to aid climbing in the most difficult areas. Camp II was installed halfway up the icefall, and Camp III was established at its top.

Above the icefall, the climbers bolted together 3 aluminum ladders, each 6 feet (1.8 m) long, to serve as a makeshift bridge across a 16-foot-wide (5 m) crevasse. On the other side of the crevasse was a valley known as the Western Cwm (*KOOM*). Sweating in the intense sunlight reflected off the Cwm's glacier, the members of the expedition wound their way through hidden crevasses. Here, Hillary and Tenzing roped together for the first time (the rope ensured that if one man fell, the other would catch him) and discovered that they made a good team.

In the middle of the Western Cwm, the climbers set up Camp IV, or Advance Base Camp, from which further work on the mountain would be carried out. The next section of the route, leading up the steep, icy face of Lhotse, was forged by Lowe, Westmacott, and Band, along with Sherpas Ang Nyima and Annullu. The hard work of cutting steps into sheer ice at such altitudes was complicated by bad weather, and it was more than a week before the route was completed. Finally, the team reached the top of the Lhotse face and descended slightly onto the South Col, a large plateau—or high, flat plain—separating the peaks of Lhotse and Everest. At 26,000 feet (7,925 m), the South Col's icy, rock-strewn surface was almost constantly pummeled by hurricane-force winds. On this barren plain, Camp VIII was established (camps V, VI, and VII having been set up on the Lhotse face). More than 700 pounds (318 kg) of gear had to be hauled to this high camp by the climbers and 17 Sherpas.

By May 26, everything was ready for the first summit attempt. Earlier, Hunt had announced that Bourdillon and Evans would make up the first summit team, with the goal of reaching the South Summit (about 300 feet, or 91 m, below the true summit). They would be followed by Hillary and Tenzing, the strongest, most acclimatized members of the group, who would try to reach the top. On the 26th, Bourdillon and Evans set out from the South Col for the South Summit, using the still-experimental closed-circuit oxygen system. That same day, Hillary and Tenzing ascended to the South Col, where they greeted an exhausted—but successful—Bourdillon and Evans.

EXPEDITION JOURNAL

Edmund Hillary
May 29, 1953

I really felt now that we were going to get to the top and that nothing would stop us. I kept frequent watch on our oxygen consumption and was encouraged to find it at a steady rate. I continued on, cutting steadily and surmounting bump after bump and CORNICE *after cornice looking eagerly for the summit. It seemed impossible to pick it and time was running out. Finally I cut around the back of an extra large hump and then on a tight rope from Tenzing I climbed up a gentle snow ridge to its top. Immediately it was obvious that we had reached our objective. It was 11:30 A.M. and we were on top of Everest!*

Now it was Hillary and Tenzing's turn. On May 27, high winds and drifting snow pinned them to the camp on the South Col, but the next day they were ready to begin their summit assault. At 7:30 A.M., they met with Gregory, Lowe, and Ang Nyima, the support team that would help them carry gear to a final camp below the South Summit. All five climbers were using open-circuit oxygen and carrying loads of 40 to 50 pounds (18–23 kg), which would increase to 60 pounds (27 kg) after they picked up additional supplies that had been dropped for them by Bourdillon and Evans's team. The support team set off first, breaking a trail in order to allow the summit pair to conserve their energy for the final push. About an hour later, Hillary and Tenzing followed, climbing almost straight up to the southeast ridge of the mountain more than 1,000 feet (305 m) above the South Col. Here, they caught up with their support team, and the five men mounted the narrow snow- and rock-covered ridge together, with steep slopes plunging down on either side of them.

Before setting off from Advance Base Camp, Hillary and Tenzing double-checked each other's oxygen equipment.

At 27,900 feet (8,504 m), they decided to set up Camp IX on a small ledge. As the support team headed back down the mountain, Hillary and Tenzing carved out two small shelves—each only six and a half feet (2 m) long and three feet (1 m) wide—across which they set up their tent. Finally, after laboring for several hours, they crawled into the tent and ate chicken noodle soup, tinned apricots, sardines, biscuits, and dates. They also drank plenty of hot lemonade-flavored water and coffee to keep from becoming dehydrated. Then Tenzing lay on the bottom ledge of the tent, almost hanging out over the sheer rock face below, while Hillary scrunched himself onto the top ledge. For two

Although Hillary and Tenzing had not met prior to the 1953 expedition, they quickly formed a bond built on mutual respect.

separate two-hour periods, they used the sleeping sets of oxygen, which allowed them to sleep for at least a little while; the rest of the time they were cold and miserable in the -17 °F (-27 °C) tent.

Finally, dawn broke. At 4:00 A.M., the two men peered outside to see that weather conditions were perfect for climbing. After drinking some more lemonade water and eating a few biscuits, they put on every piece of clothing they had with them and thawed Hillary's boots (which had frozen during the night) over the cooking stove. By 6:30 A.M., they had strapped their crampons to their boots and their oxygen tanks to their backs and were ready to set out for the summit.

1953 EVEREST EXPEDITION PROFILE: JOHN HUNT

Born on June 22, 1910, in India (then part of the BRITISH EMPIRE), John Hunt began climbing mountains at the age of 15. During the 1930s, he served with the British army in India and took part in expeditions to the Himalayas. During World War II (1939–45), Hunt served in Egypt, Italy, and Greece and also taught classes in mountain and snow warfare. After being knighted for his leadership of the 1953 British expedition to Mount Everest, Hunt returned to the army, serving until 1956. From 1963 to 1966, he served as head of the University of Aberdeen in Scotland, before becoming chairman of the Parole Board for England and Wales. Hunt also continued climbing after the Everest expedition, taking part in several expeditions around the world, including others in the Himalayas. He died in 1998.

On Top of the World

From Camp IX, Hillary and Tenzing began to work their way up the steep, narrow ridge toward the South Summit. Taking turns leading, Hillary and Tenzing struggled upward through "breakable crust"—a thin crust of snow that supported their weight for only a few seconds before sending them staggering into the powdery snow beneath. As they neared the South Summit, 800 feet (244 m) above Camp IX, the ridge widened but became steeper, requiring Hillary and Tenzing to climb almost vertically. The slope's loose snow often sent them sliding dangerously backwards. At 9:00 A.M., they reached the top of this slope and stepped with relief onto the South Summit.

After only 10 minutes, they set out again. To their left was a sheer rock precipice dropping 8,000 feet (2,438 m) into the Western Cwm, while on the right, snow cornices overhung a 10,000-foot (3,048 m) drop to the Kangshung Glacier. While one person climbed, the other wrapped the rope that joined them together around his ice ax, which he dug into the snow to serve as an anchor in case the climber slipped. About halfway between the South Summit and the true summit, Hillary and Tenzing came to a 40-foot-high (12 m) rock. Rather than climbing straight up the rock, which would have been nearly impossible at such an altitude, Hillary wedged himself into a crack between the rock and an overhanging ice cornice. Then he wiggled and JAMMED his way to the top, grabbing the rock with his hands and stabbing his crampons into the ice behind him. Tenzing followed Hillary up what is now known as the Hillary Step. Beyond the rock,

Carrying packs that weighed about 30 pounds (13.6 kg), Tenzing and Hillary were ready to begin the last stage of the climb on May 29.

the pair scaled a series of snowy humps, and finally, just as both were wondering if they would ever reach the top, they looked up to see open sky ahead of them.

At 11:30 A.M., Hillary and Tenzing stepped onto the snowy, dome-shaped summit of Mount Everest. Hillary turned to shake hands with Tenzing, who threw his arms around his partner in an exuberant hug. Then Hillary took off his oxygen mask, proving that human beings could survive at such altitudes without supplementary oxygen (no one had known if this was possible before). As sharp ice crystals borne on the wind stung his face, Hillary pulled out his camera and took a snapshot of Tenzing standing on the summit and holding up his ice ax, with the flags

Since Hillary was the only one of the pair familiar with working a camera, he photographed Tenzing standing atop the mountain.

EXPEDITION JOURNAL

George Lowe
letter home, May 31, 1953

*D*on't imagine our band of thirteen rolling and rollicking in an ecstasy brought on by victory. If you were at Base Camp now you would see nine sahibs [the Sherpa word for foreign members of an expedition] and about fifteen Sherpas lying listlessly around the tents with bloodshot and glazed eyes, thin, dirty and bewildered. Ed [Hillary] is now sleeping as he has done for hours and hours. Charles [Evans] is just smoking and tired; the talk is very desultory and dull; everyone is quite played out.... Two days ago we were on the South Col urging ourselves to the very limit—and now like pricked balloons all our reserves are gone.

NEWS CHRONICLE

No. 33,381   TUESDAY, JUNE 2, 1953   PRICE 1½d.

THE CROWNING GLORY: EVEREST IS CLIMBED

THE
QUE
DR
TOD

Back

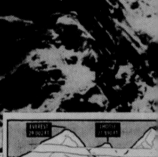

Tremendous news for the Queen

HILLARY DOES IT

GLORIOUS Coronation Day news! Everest—Everest the unconquerable — has been conquered. And conquered by men of British blood and breed.

The news came late last night that Edmund Hillary and the Sherpa guide, Tensing, of Colonel Hunt's expedition had climbed to the summit of Earth's highest peak, 29,002 feet high.

Queen Elizabeth the Second, resting on the eve of her crowning, was immediately told that this brightest jewel of courage and endurance had been added to the Crown of British endeavour. It is understood that a message of royal congratulation was sent to the climbers.

Announcers broke into U.S. radio and television programmes last night to relay the news.

Hillary, a 34-year-old New Zealander, and Bhotia Tensing, 38-year-old leader of the Sherpa guides and porters, are said to have made the final 1,000-foot ascent from Camp Eight on the upper slopes.

The feat was apparently accomplished on Monday. A year ago Bhotia Tensing climbed to within 800 feet of the summit with Raymond Lambert, of the successful Swiss expedition.

NEWS BY RUNNER

The latest news of the progress of the expedition hitherto—despatched by runner and received in London yesterday—was that the climbers were ready, as soon as the weather was suitable, to set out from Camp Seven, established high on the South Col at about 26,000 feet, to pitch Camp Eight high up near the summit.

Doreg Welker, below, describes how the conquest is likely to have been accomplished.

The two figures are in wind-proof smocks of different colours, double-lined with nylon, and each wears two hoods, beneath the visors the eyes peer out on the roof of the world to goggles greased against frosting.

Down to the right lies Tibet and to the left Nepal, while all in a variety of forms, some pleasant, lurks on every side.

At such a height no man can survive without extra oxygen. A year ago, of dead weight, where every ounce can count, at this stage science must supply what nature will not give. The endurance-time of this oxygen, carried on the back in cylinders, is estimated at five hours.

Hands are kept in three sets of gloves: outer gauntlets of windproof cotton, some mittens made of down. Next to the hands are gloves of silk.

The new Elizabethan

EDMUND HILLARY, whose conquest of Everest sets the seal on the new Elizabethan age, is a 34-year-old bee farmer from New Zealand.

He learned his mountaineering in the Alps of the little Dominion and was a pioneer in introducing winter ski-ing there.

Hillary's rugged independence made him one of this expedition's most valuable members long before the final assault.

He and George Lowe, the other New Zealander of the party, were making a free-lance climb in the Himalayas when Eric Shipton's Everest-probing expedition arrived in 1951 to choose a route up Everest. Hillary and Lowe dropped their own project and trailed halfway across the vast range to join them. Shipton was so impressed by their performance that he gave them their places in the Coronation year attempt. Shipton said last night: "This is splendid. Once the South Col camp was established there was nothing to stop them, and I have been waiting for the good news."

SMILING, mountain - wise Bhotia Tensing, is the leader of the Sherpa guides and porters who accompanied the expedition.

He is 38 and a veteran of four previous attempts on Everest by the northern route. His Sherpa comrades call him the Tiger.

On May 29 last year Tensing climbed to 28,215 feet with Raymond Lambert of the unsuccessful Swiss expedition before the failure of their...

Prophet Vicky

Here the forecast is rain—hail—sun—storm, BUT the crowds are singing in the rain SO—

WHO CARES NOW IF IT SNOWS?

CORONATION DAY FORECAST: Northerly winds, sunny spells, showers with hail and thunder, cold. Mid-day temperature 55 deg.

NEWS CHRONICLE REPORTERS

REPEATED heavy showers lashed the packed campers lining the Royal Way last night—and the temperature dropped 13 degrees in a few hours.

Yet the drenched campers refused to quit for fear of losing their places—and moment by moment the throng grew as 18,000 cars an hour converged on London. And the trains had yet to come. . . .

Thousands of cheering people surrounded the Queen Mother and Princess Margaret as they drove from Buckingham Palace after spending two hours with the Queen in her private apartments—a last visit before the Coronation.

Reinforced police could not clear a way; the car was halted for 15 minutes beside the Victoria Memorial.

The Queen Mother, in a white feathered gown and off-the-face white hat, and Princess Margaret, in a low-cut smoke-blue gown, waved. Motor-cycle police came to the rescue. But a little later more crowds ran from their pitches and blocked the route to Clarence House.

DAMP DANCES IN THE MALL

The Mall looked like a gigantic refugee camp. Over 30,000 people were bedding down along the pavements. Twenty-thousand more were trying to find places.

Thousands sat in puddles of water hanging out their clothes.

Camping up to 12-deep on either side after squatting there all day they were thoroughly soaked by the intermittent storms. But not one gave up his pitch.

Of all ages, from toddlers to over-70s, they sheltered as best they could, some under improvised tents of tarpaulin slung between the trees.

Groups were singing, others dancing in impromptu fancy dress. Quieter parties listened to portable radios or played cards. A chain of mobile cafes issued tea, coffee and buns.

It was the same among the 6,000-7,000 camped out along Whitehall.

They seemed to have thought of everything. If the sun shines today—well, some had brought seawater. If it gets very cold? There were thick blankets and heavy coats.

TENT TOWN

But it was raining a slow, miserable, penetrating drizzle. And from Trafalgar Square to Parliament Square the kerbs were lined with people huddled under tarpaulins, blankets, newspapers, umbrellas—

400 watch sea rescue

Watched by her 400 passengers, three brothers were taken aboard the Isle of Man steamer Snaefell from their crippled sailing boat, in a storm eight miles off the island yesterday.

The brothers, Christopher, Frank and Ian Whipp, of Rochdale, had ridden the storm which demasted their sloop, for 12 hours.

After the brothers had been taken aboard the steamer in heavy seas Douglas lifeboat took the sloop in tow.

Stabbed girl dead in Thames

A MURDERED girl was found in the Thames yesterday; and last night the police feared her girl companion had been killed too.

The girl in the river was 16-year-old Barbara Songhurst, a chemist's assistant, of Princess Road, Teddington. She was stabbed three times in the back after being assaulted on Lower Towpath at Ham, Surrey.

On Sunday Barbara went cycling with her friend, 18-year-old Christina Reed, of Roy Crescent, Hampton Hill.

See Page Five

Flash k cricke

Lightning struck ters dead at a match yesterday through the dre a soap factory's Irlam, near Manch

The men killed Taylor, 44, Herbe 39, and George Pea Cadishead.

CENTRAL WEATHER.—S
short sunny interv temp. 50-55. Sun a.m.-8.18 a.m. t p.m.-2.49 a.m. so water at London a.m.-5.54.

Weather map

of the United Nations, India, Nepal, and Britain streaming from its handle. Then Hillary snapped pictures of the view from the top. To the north was the dry plateau of Tibet, while to the east, the men could look down on the peaks of other Himalayan giants such as Makalu, Kanchenjunga, and Lhotse. Digging a hole in the snow of the summit, Tenzing left a small bag of sweets for the gods he believed lived on the mountain, while Hillary left a crucifix Hunt had given to him. By 11:45, the two were ready to tackle the long descent.

The achievement of reaching the top of the world was viewed as a triumph for the entire nation of Britain and its new queen, Elizabeth II.

Hillary and Tenzing began to make their way carefully down the narrow summit ridge. Following the tracks they had made on the way up, they found the journey down much easier, and by 2:00 P.M. they had arrived back at Camp IX. They rested there briefly before heading back to the South Col, where they spent the night with their support team. The next day, they continued down the mountain to rejoin the rest of the party, who had already descended to Advance Base Camp. When the other members of the expedition realized that Hillary and Tenzing had been successful, they ran out to greet the pair with hugs and congratulatory slaps on the back. Within a few hours, James Morris, the expedition's special correspondent from *The Times* of London, was on his way to communicate the news to the world. Hillary, who had been sure the achievement would interest only mountaineers, was stunned to turn on the radio at Base Camp a couple of days later and hear announcers on the British Broadcasting Corporation (BBC) network declare that Everest had at last been summited.

After nearly two months on the mountain, the expedition members descended to Tengboche, where they enjoyed the "thick" air and rested before the journey back to Kathmandu. When they finally arrived in the Nepalese capital in mid-June, they were astounded by the huge crowds waiting to greet them. Hillary and Tenzing were also shocked that most people wanted to know who had stepped on the summit first. The thought had never occurred to any of the other climbers, who thought of the two men as a team. Hillary and Tenzing agreed to say that they had reached the summit "almost together." (In his 1955 autobiography, Tenzing decided to put an end to the question: Hillary had stepped on the summit a few feet ahead of him.) From Kathmandu, the

In early July 1953, Hillary, Hunt, and Tenzing held a press conference at the Royal Geographical Society's headquarters to explain the ascent.

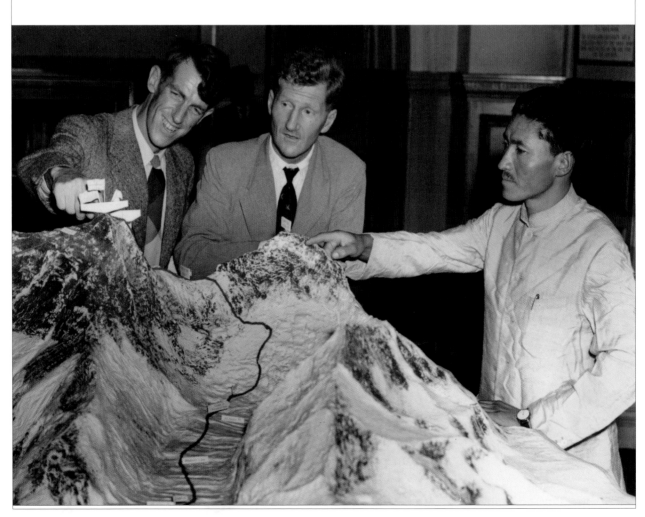

1953 EVEREST EXPEDITION PROFILE:
TOM BOURDILLON

Tom Bourdillon, who was born in London on March 16, 1924, served as president of the Oxford University Mountaineering Club (which was founded, in part, by his father) while studying physics at the school. During World War II, he served in Greece and Egypt, and afterward he worked on rocket design for the British government. Bourdillon took part in the 1951 British reconnaissance expedition to Mount Everest and a 1952 expedition to the peak of Cho Oyu in the Himalayas. Together with his father, Dr. Robert Bourdillon, he designed the closed-circuit oxygen system that he and Evans used on their climb to the South Summit during the 1953 expedition. Three years later, on July 29, 1956, Bourdillon was killed in a climbing accident on the Jägihorn, a 10,518-foot (3,206 m) peak in Switzerland.

expedition members traveled to India and then to London, where they were greeted as heroes and honored at formal receptions. They met Queen Elizabeth II, who knighted Hillary and Hunt and presented Tenzing with the George Medal, Britain's highest civilian award for bravery.

In the years after their successful ascent of the world's highest peak, both Hillary and Tenzing returned to the Himalayas, though neither ever again climbed Everest. Tenzing served as a director at the Himalayan Mountaineering Institute in Darjeeling,

Famous French climber Chantal Mauduit attempted Everest in 1993 without the use of oxygen but with modern aids such as fixed ladders.

India, while Hillary set up the Himalayan Trust to build schools and hospitals for the Sherpas of Nepal, whom he visited often. The Sherpa porters had worried that once Everest had been summited there would be no work for them, but they found themselves busier than ever, as people from around the world traveled to Nepal to make their own attempts on the huge peak.

Today, hundreds of people try to scale Everest every year, and as of 2010, about 3,000 climbers had reached the summit (many more than once), most of them aided by the fixed ropes and ladders that now line much of the route up the southern side of the mountain. With up to 75 people working their way to the peak in a single day, it can be hard to remember that Mount Everest's summit was once untrodden—and that two men were responsible for opening Chomolungma to the world.

TIMELINE

1914 — Tenzing Norgay is born in May to a Sherpa family from the Nepalese village of Thami.

1919 — Edmund Hillary is born in Auckland, New Zealand, on July 20.

1921 — The British mount the first-ever expedition to Mount Everest, exploring the mountain from the north side.

1922 — The second British Everest expedition reaches an altitude of 27,300 feet (8,321 m) on May 23, and seven Sherpas later die in an avalanche.

1924 — On June 8, George Mallory and Andrew Irvine disappear near the summit during the third British Everest expedition.

1933 — The fourth British expedition to Everest fails to climb much higher than the 1922 expedition.

1935 — In July, Tenzing Norgay joins the fifth British expedition to Everest as a porter.

1936 — In May, the sixth British expedition, again with Tenzing as porter, is forced off Everest by bad weather.

1938 — During the seventh British expedition, Tenzing and other members are caught in an avalanche but survive.

1947 — Tenzing leads Canadian-born Briton Earl Denman on an illegal attempt to climb Everest from the north.

1948 — On January 30, Hillary makes the first-ever successful ascent of the south ridge of Mount Cook in New Zealand.

1950 — A British-American expedition becomes the first to approach Everest from the south, through Nepal.

1951 — In May, Hillary makes his first trip to the Himalayas.

1951 — In September, Hillary joins the British reconnaissance mission to Everest, which spots a potential route up the mountain.

1952 — On May 28, Tenzing and Swiss climber Raymond Lambert reach about 28,000 feet (8,534 m) on Everest.

1952 — Hillary takes part in a training mission to the Himalayas in May and June, scaling several new peaks.

1952 — On September 11, John Hunt is invited to lead the 1953 British expedition to Everest.

1953 — The British expedition, along with hundreds of porters, begins the trek from Kathmandu to Everest on March 10.

1953 — Hillary and Tenzing rope together for the first time on April 26.

1953 — On May 14, most expedition members move to Advance Base Camp on the Western Cwm.

1953 — Charles Evans and Tom Bourdillon reach the South Summit of Everest, at 28,700 feet (8,748 m) on May 26.

1953 — At 11:30 A.M. on May 29, Hillary and Tenzing reach Everest's summit, at 29,035 feet (8,850 m).

ENDNOTES

AIR PRESSURE: downward pressure caused by the weight of the atmosphere, or air; at lower altitudes, the layer of air above is thicker, so air pressure is greater there than it is at higher altitudes

ALPINE CLUB: the first-ever club for mountaineers, founded in 1857 in London to promote the development of the sport and organize mountain-climbing expeditions

BRITISH EMPIRE: a group of colonies and territories around the world controlled by Great Britain from the late 1500s to the mid-1900s

BUDDHISM: an Asian religion based on the teachings of the Buddha, who held that by denying worldly desires, one could reach a state of enlightenment called nirvana

CEREBRAL EDEMA: a condition in which excessive fluid in the brain causes swelling, resulting in trouble walking and hallucinations; it can sometimes lead to death, if the victim is not immediately moved to a lower altitude

CORNICES: overhanging masses of snow or ice, often formed by the wind on mountain ridges

CRAMPONS: metal spikes fastened onto climbing boots to provide grip on ice and snow

GLACIER: a large, slow-moving mass of ice and snow that forms in mountains and in regions where more snow falls than can melt each year

JAMMED: climbed by wedging one's hands, feet, arms, and legs into any available cracks

MOLECULES: the smallest units of a substance that retain the characteristics of that substance

RECONNAISSANCE: a preliminary investigation or exploration to obtain information

ROYAL GEOGRAPHICAL SOCIETY: an organization founded in 1830 in London to support geographical research, education, and expeditions

SURVEYED: made measurements of a land area for the purposes of making a detailed map

WESTERNERS: people from the western part of the world, particularly Europe and North America

SELECTED BIBLIOGRAPHY

Clark, Liesl. *Everest: 50 Years on the Mountain*. DVD. Washington, D.C.: National Geographic Television & Film, 2003.

Coburn, Broughton. *Everest: Mountain Without Mercy*. Washington, D.C.: National Geographic Society, 1997.

Douglas, Ed. *Tenzing: Hero of Everest*. Washington, D.C.: National Geographic Society, 2003.

Hillary, Edmund. *Nothing Venture, Nothing Win*. New York: Coward, McCann & Geoghegan, 1975.

——. *View from the Summit*. New York: Pocket Books, 1999.

Hunt, John. *The Ascent of Everest*. Seattle, Wash.: The Mountaineers, 1998.

Johnston, Alexa. *Reaching the Summit: Edmund Hillary's Life of Adventure*. New York: DK Publishing, 2005.

Tenzing Norgay, with James Ramsey Ullman. *Tiger of the Snows: The Autobiography of Tenzing of Everest*. New York: G. P. Putnam's Sons, 1955.

FOR FURTHER READING

Masoff, Joy. *Everest: Reaching for the Sky*. New York: Scholastic Reference, 2002.

Platt, Richard. *Everest: Reaching the World's Highest Peak*. New York: DK Publishing, 2000.

Ramsay, Cynthia Russ. *Sir Edmund Hillary & the People of Everest*. Kansas City: Andrews McMeel Publishing, 2002.

Skreslet, Laurie. *To the Top of Everest*. Tonawanda, N.Y.: Kids Can Press, 2001.

INDEX

1921 British expedition *8, 11, 15, 44*

1922 British expedition *11, 44*

1924 British expedition *11, 12, 44*
  disappearance of Mallory and Irvine *11, 44*
  record altitude reached *11, 12*

1930s British expeditions *12, 15, 17, 44*

1951 British expedition *15, 17, 27, 41, 44*

1953 British expedition *7, 9, 15, 17–18, 19, 20, 22, 27–28, 30, 32, 33, 35, 37, 39, 40, 41, 43, 44*
  acclimatization period *22*
  camps *9, 19, 22, 27, 28, 30, 35, 37, 39, 44*
  conditions *18, 20, 28, 30, 32*
  dates *22, 28, 44*
  establishing routes *27, 28, 30*
  objectives *15, 27*
  porters *9, 18, 22, 28, 44*
  preparation for *18, 20*
  return *40, 43*
  supplies *20, 22, 27, 28, 30*

Band, George *17, 22, 27, 28*

Bourdillon, Tom *17, 28, 30, 41, 44*
  biographical details *41*

cornices *29, 35*

Denman, Earl *17, 44*

Evans, Charles *17, 28, 30, 37, 41, 44*

glaciers *22, 27, 35*

Great Britain *7, 17, 33, 39, 41, 43*

Gregory, Alfred *17, 30*

Hillary, Edmund *7, 9, 13, 15, 17, 19, 22, 27, 28, 29, 30, 32, 35–36, 37, 39, 40, 43, 44*
  biographical details *13, 44*

founder of Himalayan Trust *13, 43*
  summit ascent *30, 32, 35–36, 44*
  summit descent *39*
  writings *9, 29*

Himalayan Committee *17*

Himalayan Mountaineering Institute *23, 43*

Himalayas *7, 8, 11, 13, 17, 22, 28, 33, 39, 41, 43, 44*
  Lhotse *22, 28, 39*
  Nuptse *22*

Hunt, John *17, 27, 28, 33, 39, 43, 44*
  biographical details *33*
  selection of expedition members *17*

India *8, 11, 23, 33, 39, 43*
  Darjeeling *11, 23, 43*

Irvine, Andrew *11, 44*

Khumbu Icefall *15, 27*

Lambert, Raymond *15, 44*

Lowe, George *9, 17, 22, 28, 30, 37*

Mallory, George *11, 44*

Morris, James *17, 39*

Nepal *7, 8, 11, 12, 13, 15, 22, 23, 39, 40, 43, 44*
  Kathmandu *22, 40, 44*
  Tengboche Monastery *22, 40*

Noyce, Wilfrid *17*

number of successful summits *43*

Pugh, Griffith *17*

Sherpas *7, 9, 11, 13, 17–18, 22, 23, 27, 28, 30, 37, 43, 44*
  Ang Namgyal *27*
  Ang Nyima *28, 30*
  Annullu *28*

involvement in climbing expeditions *9, 11, 18, 22, 23, 43, 44*
  lifestyle *7, 13*
  name for Everest *7, 43*

Shipton, Eric *15*

South Col *28, 30, 37, 39*

South Summit *28, 30, 35, 41, 44*
  Hillary Step *35*

Stobart, Tom *17*

Tenzing Norgay *7, 9, 15, 17–18, 19, 23, 27, 28, 29, 30, 32, 35–36, 39, 40, 43, 44*
  biographical details *23, 44*
  role as sirdar *17–18*
  summit ascent *30, 32, 35–36, 44*
  summit descent *39*
  writings *19, 40*

Tibet *7, 8, 12, 39*

Ward, Michael *17*

Western Cwm *27, 28, 44*

Westmacott, Michael *17, 22, 27, 28*

World War II *12, 33, 41*

Wylie, Charles *17*